Other titles in the UWAP Poetry series (established 2016)

Autobiochemistry

Tricia Dearborn

Tricia Dearborn is a Sydney poet, writer and editor. Her two previous collections of poetry are *The Ringing World* and *Frankenstein's Bathtub*.

Her work has been widely published in Australian literary journals, as well as in the UK, the US, Ireland, New Zealand and online. It has also been featured in significant anthologies such as *Contemporary Australian Poetry*, *Australian Poetry since 1788* and *The Best Australian Poems* 2012 and 2010.

She is on the editorial board of *Plumwood Mountain*, an online journal of ecopoetry and ecopoetics, and was guest poetry editor of the February 2016 issue.

Dearborn is a peer assessor for the Australia Council, and has been an invited reader and panellist at many literary events, including the Sydney Writers' Festival, the Queensland Poetry Festival and Sydney Ideas. She has been awarded four grants by the Australia Council, and a Residential Fellowship at Varuna, the Writers' House.

She is a judge of the University of Canberra Vice-Chancellor's International Poetry Prize 2019, which awards a first prize of $15,000 for a single poem.

She has a BSc in Chemistry and Biochemistry, with honours in Biochemistry, and an MA in Women's and Gender Studies, specialising in literature. She loves reading, red wine, Bach and travelling, especially night journeys on sleeper trains.

Tricia Dearborn
Autobiochemistry

Poetry

First published in 2019 by
UWA Publishing
Crawley, Western Australia 6009
www.uwap.uwa.edu.au

UWAP is an imprint of UWA Publishing
a division of The University of Western Australia

THE UNIVERSITY OF
WESTERN
AUSTRALIA

ISBN: 978-1-76080-022-2

A catalogue record for this
book is available from the
NATIONAL LIBRARY OF AUSTRALIA   National Library of Australia

Designed by Becky Chilcott, Chil3
Typeset in Lyon Text by Lasertype
Printed by McPherson's Printing Group

This project has been assisted by the Australian
Government through the Australia Council, its arts
funding and advisory body.

 uwapublishing

For Cynthia, again

And for Jane

Contents

A chalk outline of the soul

Sister Pascal sketched on the blackboard
a human soul
her impromptu rendition —
which I believed anatomically exact —
shaped like a vertical dog's bone
but wider at the bottom and more angular.

She dotted it with chalk
which was original sin
then removed each smutch with the duster
which was God's grace
as manifested in baptism, marriage —
in all the seven sacraments.

That was the year I learnt
how you made words with letters,
imbibed the way their patterns
created sound and meaning, divined
that in spite of this some words
conformed to no rule but their own.

While Sister Pascal taught God's grace —
the one route to redemption —
as chrism, wedding band,
Eucharist, a small white moon
on a silver salver,
quietly I married the word.

Autobiochemistry

```
┌─────────────┐
│ 1           │
│             │
│      H      │
│             │
│   Hydrogen  │
└─────────────┘
```

Most of earth's hydrogen is not free
in the atmosphere, diatomic,

but tethered to oxygen, in water —
the human body's solvent.

Conceived in oozing warmth
we grow in a sealed-off sea.

Once born,
we require regular watering;

in the name of homoeostasis
our bodies regularly wring us out.

Besieged by infant need,
surprised by sorrow, laughter, eros,

we brim, we drip.

```
┌─────────────────┐
│ 6               │
│                 │
│      C          │
│                 │
│   Carbon        │
└─────────────────┘
```

Carbon's multivalence, its
chemical conviviality

links it into chains and rings,
improbable larger structures.

It's the skeleton of DNA,
of the hormones that make us

female, male; the sugars
that sweeten a mother's milk;

the alcohol good fortune's
toasted with. It cycles constantly

between the living
and non-living.

When my body stops, its carbon
will be freed as carbon dioxide

by fire or decay
and a tree may breathe me.

7
N
Nitrogen

You're taught the gentle
identificatory waft on day one.

I learnt it again the hard way
when I unstopped a bottle

of conc. ammonia — NH_3 —
and sniffed without thinking.

My respiratory system instantly
clenched

like a sea anemone
prodded by an inquisitive finger.

I steadied myself against
the laboratory bench,

tear-blinded, to wait it out
ashamed to admit that

through error
I could not breathe.

8
O
Oxygen

From five, I periodically
gasped for it.

The asthma medicine
would not stay down.

Relief by suppository
was slow, and greasy.

Until the day
the doctor injected me

on the ocean-green
polyester couch

and I lay shaken
by my own heart's beating

hauling in triumphant
catch after catch of air.

9
F
Fluorine

We stand for inspection,
three in a row, mouths wide open,

clowns in a sideshow alley.
Fluoride tablets are handed out:

chalky yellow, strawberry pink.
I like the yellow. One brother

likes the pink so much
he has to have his stomach pumped.

In certain compounds, fluoride ions
protect. On its own,

the element is savage.
A jet of pure fluorine gas

will provoke into combustion
things you might think inflammable,

like glass. Steel. Water.

Na

Sodium

a metal so light it floats
a metal you can cut with a knife
a metal never found free in nature

when a shaving is pared away
sodium's cut surface
shines glorious silver

but tarnishes in seconds
that incredible lustre
transformed to the dull grey of sodium oxides

heated in air, sodium burns
with a brilliant golden-yellow flame
tossed into water, it explodes

neat sodium must be swaddled
in a nonreactive substance
stored under kerosene, under oil

I wanted to be the pure metal
solely myself, self-sufficient,
swaddled in the safety

of needing no one
now I know we're never pure
beginning as we do as admixture

a dollop
of the genetically new,
from the outset, chemically intermingled

then we separate, but never completely
even when we feel entirely alone
our mirror neurons

prove us liars, firing
when we see the other damaged
or delighted, as if it were

our hand
poked with a blunt needle
or stroked by another's hand

I grew up in a house of liars
a houseful of people
pretending to be separate

but humans are never
found free in nature
it's how we're designed — connection

as vital as oxygen
intermingled, impure
we shine

the first time I saw you
your face

downloaded onto the screen
top to bottom, line by line

the first tentative touch
of your words

was black on glowing white
our matchmaker: silicon

doped with certain chemicals
it conducts or insulates

acts as a switch
zero/one off/on no/yes

over hazelnut caipiroskas
we learnt our emails had travelled

the length of a suburb
I dropped you home

your kiss switched me on
stopped my breath

15
P
Phosphorus

At school I volunteer
to set the lab stockroom in order.
Sealed in a navy lab coat

I take inventory.
Gather for disposal
crumbling samples, mystery

solutions. Rewrite acid-rotted labels.
Re-pickle a funnel-web.
Marvel at copper's rosy gleam.

Dust the jar of white phosphorus,
a sullen chunk
stored underwater,

forcibly tamed. In time
I will escape into the air,
go up in flames.

<table>
<tr><td>16</td></tr>
<tr><td>S</td></tr>
<tr><td>Sulphur</td></tr>
</table>

Cabbage, skunk and rotten egg gas
owe their reek to sulphur —
once called brimstone.

I saw him cloven-footed,
those days a hell of impotent will
ranged against impotent will.

Turns out we share onion insomnia, onion
gut-ache, the stench of sulphur compounds
in post-curry urine.

When *not under my roof* met *try and stop me*
I did not suspect this likeness,
chemical and intimate.

<table>
<tr><td>17</td></tr>
<tr><td>**Cl**</td></tr>
<tr><td>Chlorine</td></tr>
</table>

The faint scent in my friend's backyard
promised relief from the dry

grip of summer. Instead,
I went under, caught unawares

by a sudden slope down to the deep end.
My friend put into practice her bronze medallion —

placed my frantic hands on her shoulders,
breast-stroked to the side, where I lay

gasping, taking into my body
this fresh knowledge: catastrophe can loom

on a sunny day. Sometimes
another can save you.

<table>
<tr><td>20
Ca
Calcium</td></tr>
</table>

A flask is laid on the electronic scale
and tared to zero. I start with a small job lot,
topped up with smaller and smaller

increments. Index finger gently taps
the silver spatula's side, loosing a miniature
sheet of fine unseasonable snow.

In nature this white powder begins
as millions of tiny skeletons, compressed
by their own multitudinous weight

and the roaring bulk of the sea. Now it will buffer
the pH of the medium, allow me to cultivate
many crinkled circular sheets of mould.

I don't know why I'm growing mould.
I don't know what I will do with my life.
But watching and measuring I accrete

habits of precision, observation; learn
the power of purposeful repetition, the thrill
when the first portion added is exact.

tea is not high in essential nutrients
except for manganese, a 'dietary mineral'

chemically speaking,
tea is both a solution and a suspension
some of the compounds it contains
dissolved
and others suspended
within the transparent amber

tea the solution
can fix, can right
it flocks to emergencies — *hot sweet tea*
a tiny point of comfort
in the wilds of grief

tea the suspension
can usefully interrupt, postpone
or act as a bridge
between the day's compartments
it can span the space between us
from the first *how do you take it?*
to intimacies shared while the kettle boils

manganese is added to steel to strengthen it
it also fortifies human bones

tea can stiffen the spine, strengthen resolve

in fatigue, the stimulants tea contains
can be the necessary corrective

not just caffeine, but theobromine
and its isomer theophylline
the *theo-* here not from the Greek *theos*, god
(though a well-timed cup of tea can seem like a god-gift)
but from the Latin *thea*, tea

theobromine is one of the feel-goods in chocolate

theophylline is an asthma drug
the one time I took it
my hands trembled, my heart raced
as if the hounds of hell were after it

the molecule's potency
not contained by tea's kindness

At first I trickled, pleased
to have caught up at last. Proud to record
in my pale blue Holly Hobbie diary

chocolate cravings, mood swings, cramps.
Later, depleted, I learnt to match my losses.
Became more purely carnivore

to set in each of haemoglobin's
porphyrin rings
that central jewel of iron.

Zn

Zinc

Zinc
was the shed
that sheltered the car
that parish fundraising bought the nuns.

Corrugated, spangled
not weathered yet, in sequence,
to the oxide, the hydroxide,
the protective carbonate.

It sat on the concrete
behind the convent
that was next to the church
where I made an elephant

with my clasped hands —
my palms opening made its mouth
my fingers its ears
my left wrist and arm its trunk.

I sang *strength and protection may Thy passion be*
and imagined myself like the hymn said
deep in Thy wounds, Lord
a safe pink cave.

```
+---------------+
| 47            |
|               |
|    Ag         |
|               |
|   Silver      |
+---------------+
```

I tape to the doorframe
a black and white photo

developed and printed
with silver salts.

How is memory laid down?
How is it fixed?

Weeks later, I think
you look familiar ... The clock

ticks twice
before I recognise myself.

I return the ten-year-old's
captive gaze. Remember

looking into the lens,
deciding not to smile,

not to pretend.

<table>
<tr><td>50</td></tr>
<tr><td>Sn</td></tr>
<tr><td>Tin</td></tr>
</table>

I turn to pick up four empty cans,
turn to place them
on the narrow conveyor belt.

The cans are steel, plated with tin.
Pure tin, when deformed,
makes a sound — the 'tin cry'.

It will do this over and over
until it snaps. Another day,
another line. I check the code

on the top of each can.
Reject the non-conformers
and the dented, where tin's

crucial seal might be ruptured.
Three times a day
the machines grind to silence.

While others seek coffee,
sustenance, chat,
I chain smoke in the toilet.

Next year I'll implode. My life's
shiny surface breached,
revealing the old corrosion.

<table>
<tr><td>55
Cs
Caesium</td></tr>
</table>

A commercial grade caesium clock
is the size of a suitcase. It works

by a kind of ticking you can't hear:
the jump of caesium 133's

55th electron — footloose
above the cloistered 54 —

to a higher orbit. Beyond
precise, this atomic sundial.

Accurate to within a second
in 1.4 million years.

Sometimes after what seems aeons
a decision is made

in an instant unmeasurable
even by the caesium clock.

A woman kisses you.
You make the leap.

<table>
<tr><td>74</td></tr>
<tr><td>**W**</td></tr>
<tr><td>Tungsten</td></tr>
</table>

sudden dusk
in the house again
my hand at the light switch

it's always one of those
old black bakelite switches
that click so distinctly

click! the filament
fails to blaze, an ominous
absence of incandescence

I run from switch to switch
each click! floods a room
with nightmare dark

A habit. A fever. A buoy.
My morning's
cup-of-tea-warmed shelter.

For holidays, first-packed.
What I rescue
from dream-fires.

An inconvenient accumulation,
lining too many shelves,
stuffed under my desk.

Spiral bound, perfect bound, hand
bound, skinned with vinyl,
leather, fake fur.

Repository of forgotten shocks,
disasters, epiphanies, synchronicities,
self-deceptions, moments of cautery.

Inscribed onto ivory paper
with an implement whose iridium tip
will endure intact

when ink is a ghost and paper, dust,
the minerals of my bones
reclaimed by earth.

<table>
<tr><td>79
Au
Gold</td></tr>
</table>

i.

Gold does not tarnish.
Tutankhamen's death mask glows

as on the day it was lowered
to his emptied, resined flesh.

It resists most chemical assaults.
Aqua regia, a fuming union

of savage acids, will dissolve it.
So two Nobel medals sheltered

in plain sight —
a flask of orange solution

on a high laboratory shelf
the duration of a war.

ii.

On my way into the shop, I stumble.
Bend to retrieve the impediment,

a handful of thrumming pleasure.
The owners say *nothing but trouble*.

I add the cost of her to my milk and bread.
Fed, belly comically swollen:

a paper ball chaser. Teased,
a small spitting warrior.

In scarred lip, wasted limb, matted fur,
scurfy skin, behind the cloudy

blinded eye, something immune
to the onslaught, incorruptible.

<table>
<tr><td>80</td></tr>
<tr><td>Hg</td></tr>
<tr><td>Mercury</td></tr>
</table>

I feel the thermometer's small
extra coldness slipped under my tongue,

the slow poison contained
by its sheath of glass.

Too much of the silvery liquid metal
huddles within the bulb.

You swathe me in quilts, add a beanie,
rub my feet. Observe and record

my temperature's unremitting fall.
Until you see mercury's properties

of thermal expansion at work,
the thin line creeping up past the gradations.

When I toss back the bedclothes, you say
take it slow. But I felt that internal thermostat

kick in, like a two-stroke after the cough-and-fades
when that stuttering roar takes hold.

Inorganic chemistry lab. A rack of test tubes
filled with colourless solutions.

Drops of another transparent liquid added.
In each tube, something new appears:

a precipitate, an insoluble solid,
which may be crystalline, curdy, colloidal;

may float as a flocculent mass, or plummet
brightly coloured to the bottom.

I was blind to my feelings for my friend.
One drunken night recognition bloomed.

Add a drop of lead nitrate to potassium iodide:
a canary bursts forth from a clear sky.

Covalent bonds

In America

When we visit your grandma
your accent springs out
like a joke snake from a can.

Your voice has a vigour
new to me. I watch as you plump out
with recognition, with relief.

See you for the first time
without the mask you wear
in your other homeland.

Ride

Last night we both saw things in the other
we had and hadn't suspected —

my stubborn selfishness, your willingness
when pushed to ride roughshod.

This morning my inner thighs are sore
from the hours of fucking before the fighting.

In the toilets at work I pull down my sleeve
to look at the bite mark on my shoulder.

Ride me again, resist me again, so
many ways to know each other better.

Phlegm: a love poem

I'm reading Maggie Nelson
occasionally stopping to cough up phlegm
in some indeterminate post-fever stage of the flu

she's living on a canal with a junkie boyfriend
or that's how I read it

the poems might as well be called 'no good will come of it'
raging despair oozes out of them
toxic as the canal's stinking sludge
or my almost fluorescent yellow-green phlegm

I hack
'Spit,' says my mind
I spit out on the tissue
'Good girl,' I say out loud

I learnt this

my mother, not big on emotion or touch,
excelled at sickbed ritual

earlier tonight I was telling my girlfriend
(scavenger of sleep, getting what she can between my bouts)
how it calmed me as a child, calms me now

the bucket by the bed in case you were sick
the towel laid cross-wise on the bed underneath you
in case you didn't quite get to the bucket
its strange comforting roughness
the smell of disinfectant
when the bucket came back fresh

then I instructed her in percussive therapy
another thing I learnt from my mother
it breaks up the phlegm

she pounded me on the back as I lay angled off the sofa
head resting on my forearms on the ground
up/down from the waist to the top of the shoulder blades

then helped me back onto the sofa
where I lay sweating
while she looked on with patient palpable concern

I notice we get on better when I'm sick
she less defensive and kinder
I more vulnerable, less autocratic

at night a Buteyko technique I found on the internet
eases the coughing
to begin, you take a breath
and hold it 'till discomfort'
the aim is to create *air hunger*

lately I'm learning to tolerate
the right kinds of discomfort
to honour the hungers my mother discounted

Maggie tells her boyfriend
it's not the content / I'm in love with, it's the form

how can you separate
a slender torso, small breasts, their exuberant nipples
a clitoris that is a chameleon to the tongue
now rampant, now indiscernible
somehow melded back into bone
from the love, the rightness
the great goodwill

her habits with time which are mine with money
no planning
then blaming the shortfall
on some unexpected but perfectly foreseeable circumstance

her face turned to me on the sofa
its energy and joy
dark circles under her eyes
because I've been keeping her up at night
coughing

Everything including the obvious

how can I describe you, my surprise, my unpredictable
your mind encompasses multitudes while I
am down on my knees squinting at the particular

your brain works sideways like a crab but in every direction at once
    on many levels
no point asking what you're thinking — too many things to list
though sometimes I ask you to toss me three at random

the tips of all ideas have handles, their wholenesses dangling below
you flash the handles and I learn to catch them

for the sake of internal peace you're learning to winnow
but your taste for multiplicity expands me,
flavours our life together, my habit of discernment a seasoning

by comparison I'm a slow simplistic one-track wonder
gathering towards potential actions in my steadfast cumulative
    felt-sensed way

shake it up! you say
willing to lose it all to gain it all
in your world everything including the obvious

just one of the possibilities

At last

how lucky
that I outlasted
my inability to feel loved

how lucky that I met you
in the meantime

that you were willing
to wrap your arms around
the barrier around me

to hold me
while I worked
to let go of the reasons

until unexpectedly love
came flooding in

throwing the world open

The opposite of forgetting

i.m. Pat Qua, jazz pianist, artist, next-door neighbour extraordinaire

when I arrive you know me

but I've also become
the person up the ladder doing something to the bricks in the wall
the person who left the paintings with you

wasn't it you?
it wasn't you?
it didn't have any connection with you?

the paintings are stacked
with a letter you don't remember
signed with a name
you don't remember

you say, it's like my memory's
forgotten that other person
and inserted you in there instead

I look forward to being
your first husband, both your sons

if that's what it comes to

Third-degree

The ash of your cigarette
creeps closer to scarred fingers.
Only your face escaped the fire.

You tell me you keep your shirt on
at the beach, so as not to shock.
Took it off once

hating the feeling of it
between you and the water.
But it wasn't the shirt.

You tax me with not intervening
the night your lover
tossed a glass of wine at you

then held a lighter to the blankets.
I remember the sounds
of the scuffle next door.

We don't talk of the night
he came back with a bottle of petrol
and lit you in earnest.

You pounding on my door
while I stood frozen.

Less of you

for Kerry Leves

Your tooth-grinder's ragged grin
is still so you
I'm surprised to learn walking's

one of those pleasures
you've had to forsake for good.
I note the frailness of your arms.

Each time I walk down Oxford Street
there's less of you.

But you share my caramel mud cake,
eat your half with relish.
Shout with sudden laughter

when — fishing for gossip —
I declare myself a story whore.
I won't forget you

reading 'Poppies in July' aloud
with the breath you had left.
Repeating each stanza over and over

until I sneakily herded you on.
Saying you didn't remember it being
so long.

Observe

Remember the day when the world
whirled, and the exquisite nausea
made the ambulance a torture.

And the doctor induced it —
laid you back quickly
turned your head to the side

and after seconds of
nothing much
you were on that internal Gravitron again

the room whipping around you
as you gripped the bed
and cried out in alarm.

She did it to observe
the precise rotation of your eyes,
confirm a benign diagnosis.

When the world had slowed
you hunched over the emesis bag
heaving up froth and bile.

She said, *I'll give you a minute
then we'll do the other side.*
Kindness can look like that.

Virginia Woolf's memoirs

Photograph with Father

Father's birthday. He ... could have been 96, like other
people one has known; but mercifully was not.

Diary, 28 November 1928

Sir Leslie Stephen lords it
in the foreground

grizzle-bearded, patriarchal
his gaze is turned to you

whose soft-blurred features
can't disguise

the fine straight nose
and downcast eyes

smooth wings of hair
shoulders slightly hunched

as if you dared not
breathe too deeply

while he was in focus
you could not be

The angel in the house

I see now that she was living on such an extended surface
that she had not time, nor strength, to concentrate ... upon me,
or upon anyone — unless it were Adrian.

A Sketch of the Past, 1939

Despite your singularity
her eyes, which were yours,
never saw you

in the particular.
You were one of
the many she tended

and she preferred the male —
her duty first to a fretful husband;
her joy reserved

for her youngest son.
Her minutes with you diminished further
by the claims of infirmary,

workhouse, sickbed.
You watched her give herself away,
deftly, pridefully,

piece by piece.
Knew how it felt *to want*
and want and not to have

long before what was left of her
slipped, exhausted,
into the grave.

Nessa

I always feel I'm writing more for you than for anybody.
Letter to Vanessa Bell, 15 October 1931

From the moment of that chance encounter
under the nursery table

when she asked you if black cats had tails
and you said no

she was your co-conspirator,
your best-beloved

rival — painter to your writer,
fruitful to your childless,

stoic to your voluble,
Dolphin to the Billy Goat

and later — you were often plural
in your affections — to the Apes

who hooted and wooed her.
You considered yourself her firstborn.

Demanded your 'rights' —
those kisses and pettings.

Without her you merely existed,
dry and dusty.

With her,
you would always be the child

who fingered her amethyst necklace,
naming with each bead

a person she loved,
a jealousy.

Taking the train to Maidenhead

... certainly I find the climax immensely exaggerated.
Letter to Ka Cox, 4 September 1912

After you suddenly told him
that you loved him,

that you'd marry him,
you both felt you must get away

and took the train to Maidenhead.
Leonard rowed you

up the river to Marlow,
those hours, he recollected,

like *a beautiful, vivid dream.*
Months later —

some trouble on the honeymoon,
doctors' warnings against a child.

You kept the faithful Mongoose
in your service, abandoned

certain expeditions.
There were rivers — said the doctors

Leonard listened to —
too risky to explore.

Vita

*... she shines in the grocer's shop in Sevenoaks with a
candle lit radiance, stalking on legs like beech trees, pink
glowing, grape clustered, pearl hung.*

Diary, 21 December 1925

Vita roused in you what Leonard did not.
Thrillingly aristocratic, a ship in full sail.

Sitting on your floor in her velvet jacket
as you knotted her pearls.

When she threatened to drive to Monk's House late,
throw gravel at your window and spend the night

you telegraphed: 'Come then'. She was what you
had never been — a *real woman*, controlling

silver, servants, chow dogs. But you saw
what was missing, that thing that didn't vibrate

at the core. The ardour you could not supply
she swiftly sought in other lovers.

The legacy of your affair:
enduring friendship; memories

of those nights
you did not write about.

Ethel

I get, generally, two letters daily. I daresay the old fires
of Sapphism are blazing for the last time.

Diary, 16 June 1930

In Vita's wake
what should land in your lap

but an elderly Sapphist
in a three-cornered hat.

A general's daughter —
lusty, loquacious,

persistent, deaf,
demanding

her hour of glory,
your attention, all the details.

Commanding an orchestra,
commanding the room.

You admired her gallantry
in the face of failure.

Found a new frankness
in missives for her eyes.

Deplored the tempestuous scenes
she thrived on.

Rose up indignant
against her jealous claims.

Basked in the blaze.

Freud's narcissus

Freud is upsetting; reducing one to whirlpool ...
Diary, 9 December 1939

Vita dropped you at Selfridge's
to buy a steak for your dinner guest,

Freud. When you started tunnelling
in earnest, excavating

the caves behind yourself,
a small you was spotlit

on that ledge, your half-brother's
hand under your clothes, moving

inexorably down.
By the time your imprint

published Freud, by the time
you gave him steak for dinner,

he'd recanted what he knew
of such violations, pronounced them

a child's own fantasy.
That night his gift to you

was a narcissus. You gazed
into the swirling waters.

Virginia Woolf's memoirs

At 60 I am to sit down & write my life.
Diary, 8 February 1926

At fifty-nine, you —
who had written *I can't stop looking* —

unable to close your ears
to the voices

stopped looking.
You walked to the river.

Elephant poems

The invisible elephant

it's been there nearly all my life
in the middle of the living room

in the middle of the space
where I have tried to live

tried to accommodate myself
to the way it uses up the room
breathes my air
fouls the floor

never knowing when it will block me,
trip me, grip me by the throat
and knock me down

I have felt mad
not knowing exactly where
or what it is
how to navigate around it

ashamed of this secret
burden, this unnameable impediment

by now, despite efforts to avoid it
I have bumped into it
from what feels like every possible angle

flouting shame, I have allowed others
to come up close
and test their palms against its presence

gradually
its outlines have revealed themselves

it's the shape of
stifled cries in the dark
fear of footsteps
waking in puddles

it's the shape of two worlds in one,
the shape of one world
split in two

the shape of dreams of twos —
pairs, twins, doubles, replicas
two fridges, two children, two elephants

(the elephants were frozen, I had to defrost them)

what to do with it?

eat it

I hack off invisible limbs
blood flows from the trumpeting air

I chew my way through it, down to the tusks,
the ears, and the tip of the tail

it doesn't taste good, but it tastes
real
and the room is mine

A certain kind of silence

i.

A nine-year-old stands squinting
in the post-Mass winter glare
of a big backyard

wearing a boxy woollen pantsuit
in blue and green tartan.
Her brothers are up on the swing set

playing and yelling.
The jacket has large white buttons.
The pants are lined

but the scratch comes through.
There's no point telling her mother
the pantsuit scratches,

no point telling her mother
that buttons revolt her.
Her mother knows.

ii.

You stand at a distance,
throwing me gifts.

I catch them, examine them,
put them away.

they're always thoughtful
and well-chosen.

They sit on my shelves, as quiet
as you wished me to be.

iii.

We swap insolubles
on the phone. Specify

number of letters,
spell out what's known.

Each clue a world
in its own right,

nothing extraneous
to its purpose.

Together we fill the grid,
our conversation

neatly restricted
to down and across.

iv.

A certain kind of silence is ensured
by constant chatter —
the weather, directions from A to B,

what happened on the bus today —
reinforced by the white noise
of stories I've heard so many times

the first words galvanise me
to a reflex fending-off.
But through it all,

silence prevails — as at four,
when I opened the door
from the dark hallway

and found the night-dazzling kitchen
could not hold
what I had to tell you.

Therapist, recorded

I have you
in a box on my desk.

When I click
you say what you said before

again. As many times as I want.
There is that smile

that felt like love.
There is your habit of hangnail biting

which I don't even know
if you know I know.

There you are, open to me
in your special way.

As I am to you
when you are in replay.

Static in amber

this is what I see:

my family in amber
or some substance like amber
but cloudy, and darker

not brittle like amber, either
but sticky-solid

within it, we are
obscure to each other
fixed in our places

it takes years of effort
to first get my head out

to discover, astonished,
that the world is not made of amber

then to haul myself bodily
from the viscid exudate
of my father's lies

while I very gradually
and repeatedly
escape

the others are motionless, mute

turning a trained blind eye
to the world
beyond amber

where people can be seen
through the clear air, clearly

are free
to move closer
and further away

Sanctuary

We woke to that kitchen's
good morning smell of toast

its squares of lino,
green, blue and red

that we hopscotched across,
the gas stove that leaked a little

so that, to this day, a faint smell of gas
is homey and slightly magical.

Played in the long backyard
with the old cracked path,

its lemon tree, dahlias, frangipani,
beans and mandarins, passionfruit vine.

Or in Grandpa's stone-floored garage,
always cool, with its thick dark

smell of engine oil. At night
we lay wakeful in the small wooden beds

with the built-in drawers
or on the mattress laid between them

claiming each train in turn,
each of us wanting the last of the night

to be ours, the winner announced
by a lengthening peace.

From the small recessed window
the Virgin Mary in her blue robes

watched over us, arms outstretched.
The bathroom had a noisy glass towel rail,

a high old-fashioned light switch
still out of my reach at seven.

In the sheltering night of that house
when I called out to Mum

she'd come to me
from the back verandah.

In the hallway, the child Christ clings
to a knowing-eyed Madonna.

He's run to her from his bed,
one sandal dangling.

The angels to either side
with their terrifying portents.

Jane the umbrella

I dreamt four umbrellas
two open
two closed

in daylight, I take umbrellas
from the hook in the hall

lay my unconscious out
on the lounge room floor

the red umbrella is Jane

she shelters
she opens to me
she is above me and beside me at once

I am the purple umbrella
I mimic her openness

under my spread, the two small umbrellas
each closed
in a different way

one is misshapen, ugly
packed full of feeling

the other neat, presentable,
vacant

I recognise
my small split self

Your life as a jigsaw

i.

you are a 5000-piece puzzle with unaccountable pieces missing
sometimes it's just a piece of sky
but even sky can be important

someone has taken those pieces away
a small hand holds them
the hand is yours

you can't force this fist
it has its reasons

you'll never see it open

ii.

jigsaw is the name of the puzzle
it is also
the electric saw with its fine reciprocating blade
very good for cutting curves

iii.

sometimes something bumps into the table
and the borders of the jigsaw
jackknife
and whole clumps and individual pieces scatter

sometimes
what's left is unrecognisable
until enough chunks have been slid back together
enough pieces matched
        by painstaking experiment, by guesswork, by luck

until there is enough tree, or sky, or land or water
for you to see
which way is up

iv.

a missing piece
is restored to the puzzle
that small hand moving faster than the eye can see

and a blotch becomes a face, an odd piece of brown
is a table corner, or reveals
the fish-shaped clothes brush with the stuck-on eye
that lived on your mother's dressing table
when you were four

v.

you've always known about the puzzle
even when you didn't

even in those years
when your mother had flipped a tablecloth over it
when you ate your meals off it
when you wandered blind

without the map the cuts made

The running doll

the doll in my dream
is one of those old-fashioned plastic dolls
with arms and legs that move

but this doll has no arms
no head

as it runs, its naked torso
turns rhythmically from side to side
almost as if its body
were saying no

as it turns you can see into first one
armhole then the other

the doll is hollow, its chest
empty

armless, the doll
can't push away

headless, it can't
understand or strategise

lungless, mouthless
it can't cry out

how easy to stoop and catch
a running doll, to make it
do what you want it to do

Coffee

a Christmas without family:
the price of a truth no one wants
least of all me

trouble at home
can't I shelve it for the holidays?
can't I be happy?

at the café, for the cost of a coffee
this bustling calm
the balm of welcome

Impact

why can't you ignore it
like the others

because it was you that was
bombed, shattered

because it's time to honour
this destruction

honour the fact
you were there

at the moment of impact

the moment you realised
there was no safety in daylight

no safety in numbers
no safety anywhere

the bathtub
a brother to either side

that plausible soapy hand

I text you a photo of my knitting

the knitting lies curved
along its cable
it rests on the pattern

which covers my journal
in which is secreted
my dream of two nights ago

the one where I called my father
a cunt, a *complete* cunt
then walked out of the house

can my dream, through layers
of paper and card, through wool
and plastic and steel

through the ether, via satellite
find you, transmit to you
what you've forbidden me to speak of

Therapist, dreamt

The night after the second session
we walk through spacious dream-rooms,
talking. In future instalments

you talk about Jung on the sofa at the party.
We stand at a fence, looking in at
some wild greenery.

You call me darling. Cook me pikelets.
You're pregnant.
You speak beautiful French.

I'm running late for a session and the toilet
is full of socks.
Your hair is dark when you are blonde,

you're black when you are white.
You wear a terrible cloth cap that doesn't suit you,
a hat that makes you look like Miss Marple.

You have two bloodless gashes on your face.
My glass of water
spills into your fireplace.

In the kitchen of my childhood home
I make you tea.
You're in our bathroom

where the mirror should be.
You're a terrier. You lean to nibble
the belly of the small furred creature

that wriggles luxuriously at your side.
You're in the dream with the very small plum tree
surprisingly in blossom.

We are almost always in the same country,
the same room. Once
in the same bed

where you held me safely as I slept
so my body could remember. Another time,
we strip. You're going to help me

warm the frozen person
who gripped my hand and was hauled up
from under the sand under the ocean.

A weekly harrowing

no surnames, no stories —
a shared legacy
of shame, silence, isolation

back and forth back and forth
the horses drag the harrow

wanting to disappear
is part of it: some women
learn to stay, to stand it

the slicing discs
expose small maimed creatures

unexpectedly, shame reflected
acts
as antidote

as the blades churn up the earth
its colour
deepens

learning that you are
your own thing, that the world's
yours also

backbreaking work
and never done for good

Twos

two more weeks till I can count
the number of sessions left
on just one hand

though we've yet to crack the mystery
of my dreams of twos

in last night's I was on a train
and behind us on the tracks
was another train

its light blinding me when I turned to look at it

we were pulling up at our stop
my two bags weren't closed properly,
I wasn't ready

when I ask, you say
you've never had a theory about the twos

see, I'd have been theorising
the fuck out of that shit

one of the differences between us

another being — though I can't know for sure
because whenever I see you you're working —
that I swear more than you do

I'll miss your small nose yawns
the gnawing on your hangnails
which happens less since I wrote about it

another difference being that
while we both observe
I document

but we're contemporaries, you
more distant than my brothers,
closer than my sister

both raised religious

both choristers
which I knew when you knew the difference
between a chorus and a chorale
also
the way you gleamed while I spoke of it

we both have the habit of wearing
new favourite clothes all the time
can't wear wool next to our skin

we share the same unusual middle name
though mine languishes in the otherworld
reserved for names ditched by deed poll

but the train approaches the station
I have to get my bags together

you said if we'd met a different way
we might have been great friends
and that was the cost

but now I find the cost
is the loss
of what was built to free me

Scar massage

a tiny section of my body
was excised, sent off for biopsy

a day or two later
somebody jokingly asked
how I thought my mole was going

I found I could not bear to think of
that small piece of me
floating in clear fluid in a plastic bottle
in a pathologist's office

irretrievable, irrevocably
exiled

I was left with a cavity
that has sealed itself over
with the help of two continuous sutures

now that the stitches are out and a week has gone by
I massage the scar for five minutes twice a day
using, as advised, two fingers
and as much pressure as I can tolerate
to prevent the join
hardening

I am astounded by the depth of its colour

other parts of me have been lost
other scars left to harden

these are not so visible

I have stopped ignoring them nonetheless
have stopped trying to disguise them
with complaisance, competence, facts-at-the-ready

I return to them, feel for
their shapes under the surface
attest their presence
with as much pressure as I can tolerate

I speak to them

tell them
that they are no longer alone

The change: some notes from the field

Perimenopause as rocket science

you know
the instant of ignition
because it feels like you're standing

directly under those roaring jets
no way out now
you're strapped in

pointed towards
the blue
that will become a coruscating dark

let's hope you can handle
some solid g's
as you take off

another layer, sweating
on your trajectory
to an undiscovered world

Perimenopause as the weather at sea

gone is the swell
the long slow bodily knowledge
of tides and patterns
conditions are choppy out on the water
storms blow up from nowhere

Perimenopause as my parents' radiogram

I'm out of kilter, my life a 33⅓ thrashed at 78
as we did with our parents' light operas
on the wooden radiogram
laughing until we cried
and I

who once turned majestic at the centre
of this cycling life
am forced out as it turns more quickly
out to the edge and eventually
over

as a kid, spun around and around, let go
you know what happens:
you fall down
how long will it take to get my legs
in a strangely steady world

Perimenopause as a ticket to KL

you don't need to save up
or have shots

to reach the steamy latitudes
just do the washing up

think about something
that pisses you off

walk quickly up a hill
drink a glass of red

bam! you're in Kuala Lumpur, Borneo, Bangkok
suffused with dripping heat

you don't need a plan or a passport
or even to be upright

the tropics will find you in bed

Perimenopause, in which everything is a fan

my hand,
the mouse mat, the
bedroom door, my sunhat,
the postcard from Valetta, the
freelance schedule, a saucepan lid,
my journal, the *Sydney Morning Herald*,
an emptied plate, the Queen of Cups, the
birthday card, the actual paper fan my niece
made, the page proofs, the envelope they
came in, *My Brilliant Friend*, my
lover's focused
b
r
e
a
t
h

Perimenopause as a pitched battle between the iron supplements and the flooding

These spring tides will not be stemmed.

To ward off not just anaemia
but the scalpel which would loose from me

that generative pocket
with the moon's horns

and the moon's own pattern
of increase and decay

I rally the troops:
long brown powdery tablets

with a faint taste of fenugreek.
Every six months

an aliquot of what I can least spare
is taken

to see who's winning.

Perimenopause as a chance to get a few things off my mother's chest

my mother and I are not alike
in temperament or constitution

though at twelve she told me (ruefully) I had her thighs
and at sixteen a stranger in a shop

spoke my mother's maiden name
asked was I her daughter

why do I find her grievances now curled under my tongue
her rage surging down my arms

my mother marched off
to bash the pans in the kitchen while she cooked

I storm off many times, returning
to speak and speak my dissatisfactions

which I hear and recognise as hers — neglect, lack of appreciation —
my mother threatened to throttle us

when we misbehaved
she didn't, she throttled herself

and now I speak it

Perimenopause as sweat lodge

I am a blushing bride
of transmutation, dewy-skinned
for a new reason

blanketed by the same layer
of lush, laden air
my lover fended me off from

when my palm relished
her intermittently luscious biosphere
I am a hothouse orchid

trembling on its stem
catch me ever
paying for a sauna again

Perimenopause as uncertainty and invitation

you never know when you're due
you never know whether

it's the weather, or you
rhythms of thirty years' standing

begin to stretch, compress
to split at the seams

through the gaps
stream questions, angers, revelations

nail polish in a shade of blue
you never dared

a frankness
you never dared

a mission
should you choose to accept it

to take no shit
for the rest of your life

Notes

Autobiochemistry

The resources consulted during the writing of the sequence 'Autobiochemistry' include Theodore Gray, *The Elements: A Visual Exploration of Every Known Atom in the Universe* (Black Dog & Leventhal, 2009); David L. Heiserman, *Exploring Chemical Elements and Their Compounds* (McGraw-Hill, 1992); and Hugh Aldersey-Williams, *Periodic Tales: The Curious Lives of the Elements* (Viking, 2011).

Virginia Woolf's memoirs

All epigraphs are by Virginia Woolf.

'to want and want and not to have': Virginia Woolf, *To the Lighthouse*, 1927

'dry and dusty': letter from Virginia Woolf to Vanessa Bell, 2 October 1937

'a beautiful, vivid dream': Leonard Woolf, *Beginning Again*, 1967

'real woman', 'silver, servants, chow dogs': Virginia Woolf, Diary, 21 December 1925

'I can't stop looking': Virginia Woolf, Diary, 12 October 1940

A weekly harrowing

The title is a quote from Meredith Wattison, personal communication.

Perimenopause as uncertainty and invitation

'[Your] mission, should you choose to accept it' is from the *Mission: Impossible* TV and film series.

Acknowledgements

Heartfelt thanks to the Australia Council for the Arts for a grant that supported the completion of this book. Thanks also to Varuna, the Writers' House, for a two-week Residential Fellowship at a critical juncture.

Thanks to Dr Isaac Gewirtz of the Henry W. and Albert A. Berg Collection of English and American Literature, The New York Public Library, who permitted me to view Virginia Woolf's diaries.

Thanks to my partner Cynthia Nelson, who has given these poems — sometimes through many versions — the gift of her trusted, unsparing eye. To Maggie Joel, for endless and endlessly stimulating conversations about writing and the writing life. To Debbie Duncan, for cups of tea, wine on the verandah, margaritas and talk, talk, talk. To my brothers Michael and Paul for (respectively) useful information pertaining to the use of silicon in computers and feedback on the poem '[14] Silicon'. To my nephew Sam for introducing me to the Periodic Table of Videos (www.periodicvideos.com/). Thanks also to Brady Haran for creating it, and to Martyn Poliakoff and the other chemists at the University of Nottingham who provide the content. To my nieces Georgia and Evie for expertly making me paper fans.

To Terri-ann White, the Director of UWA Publishing, for her enthusiasm and generosity, Kate Pickard for her skilful handling of contract and production matters, and publicist Charlotte Guest for her good cheer and timely reminders.

Thanks to the editors of the following journals and anthologies, in which many of the poems in this collection previously appeared: Yvonne Forward, *Attachment* (UK); Judi Blumenfeld Hoadley, *Australasian Journal of Psychotherapy*; Mark Tredinnick, *Australian Love Poems* (Inkerman & Blunt); Jill Jones and Bella Li, *Australian Poetry Anthology 2018*; Melinda Smith, *Canberra Times*; Claire Albrecht, *The Clambake: Cuplet Anthology 2018*; Keri Glastonbury, *Cordite 57: Confession*; Judith Beveridge, *Cordite 80: No Theme VI*; Nigel Featherstone, Michele Seminara and Robbie Coburn, *The Hunger: Verity La Anthology No. 1*; Philip Porter and Andy Kissane, *The Intimacy of*

Strangers: North Shore Poetry Anthology No. 2; Sarah Holland-Batt, *Island Magazine*; Jake Goetz, *Marrickville Pause*; Moya Pacey and Sandra Renew, *Not Very Quiet*, no. 1; Moya Pacey, Sandra Renew and Lisa Brockwell (guest editor), *Not Very Quiet*, no. 3; Anne Casey, *Other Terrain*; Anne Elvey, 'Poets Speaking Up to Adani' in *Plumwood Mountain*; Jack Ross, *Poetry New Zealand Yearbook 2018;* Michael Farrell (guest editor), *Rabbit: a journal for non-fiction poetry*; Stuart Barnes, *Tincture*; Heather Taylor Johnson, *Transnational Literature*; Michele Seminara and Robbie Coburn, *Verity La*; and Cassandra Atherton, *Westerly*.

'In America' was Highly Commended in the 2014 Tabor Adelaide Writing Awards.

'Everything including the obvious' was commissioned by guest editor Stuart Barnes in 2018 for *Cordite 88: TRANSQUEER*.

'Less of you' was commissioned by The Red Room Company in 2012 for *The Disappearing: Oxford Street* (smartphone app).